affirm press

First published by Affirm Press, 2024
Bunurong/Boon Wurrung Country
28 Thistlethwaite Street, South Melbourne, VIC 3205
affirmpress.com.au

Affirm Press is located on the unceded land of the Bunurong/Boon Wurrung peoples
of the Kulin Nation. Affirm Press pays respect to their Elders past and present.

13 5 7 9 10 8 6 4 2

Text and illustrations copyright © Jess Racklyeft, 2024

A catalogue record for this
book is available from the
National Library of Australia

ISBN: 9781923022812 (hardback)

Cover and internal design by Kristy Lund-White © Affirm Press
Typeset in Neutraface Text and Beatrix Plain
Printed and bound in China by RR Donnelley Asia Printing Solutions Ltd.

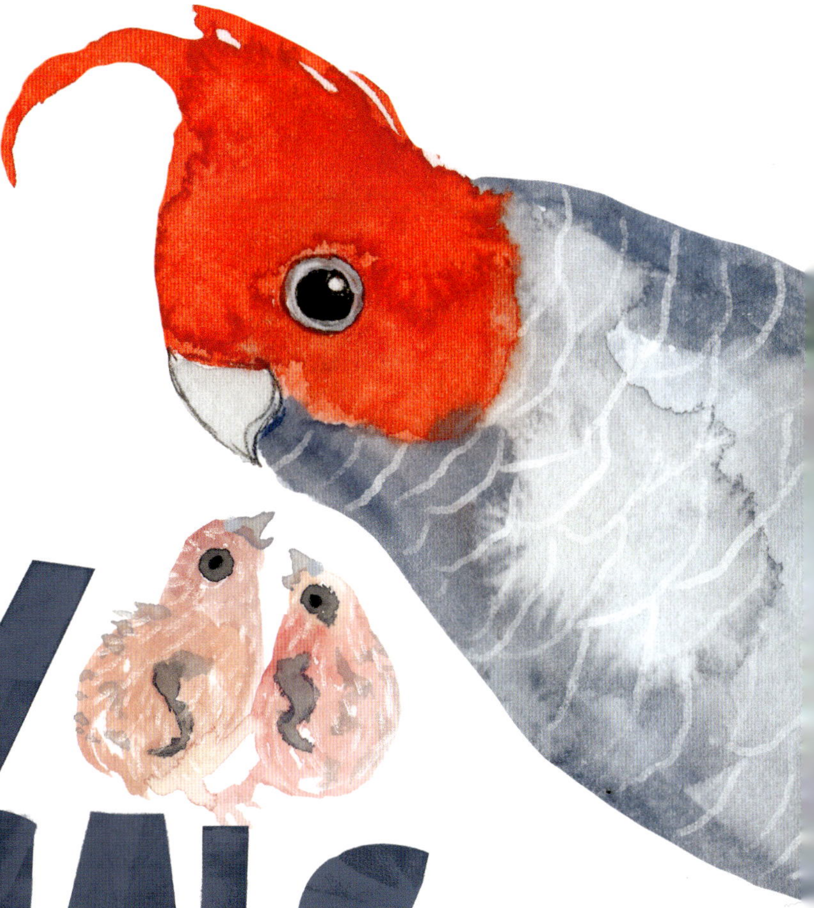

Australia's BABY ANIMALS

affirm press

There are so many incredible creatures living in Australia. They can be found in all kinds of places, growing, living and communicating in different ways.

But the one thing *every* animal has in common? They each start life as a baby!

In this book, you will learn some of the amazingly varied ways that animals begin their lives – from being born featherless and sightless, like Pied Currawong (*Strepera graculina*) hatchlings, to starting life at a whopping 4 metres long, like Humpback Whale (*Megaptera novaeangliae*) calves.

You will meet babies who mature at different speeds – some who stick by their parents for years, like the Antilopine Wallaroo (*Osphranter antilopinus*), or independent little ones who are ready to fend for themselves straight away, like the Tiger Snout Seahorse (*Hippocampus subelongatus*).

Corroboree Frog eggs

Willie Wagtail egg

Australian Kestrel egg

Intermediate Egret egg

Comb-Crested Jacana egg

Wedge-Tailed Eagle egg

Cassowary egg

You will also discover the many Australian environments that animals grow up in, across the earth and in trees, skies, rivers and seas. And you will learn how baby animals interact with these environments, from the Flatbacked Turtle (*Natator depressus*), whose sex is determined by the temperature of the sand, to the Wedge-Tailed Eagle (*Aquila audax*), who learns how to fly from a huge nest built 30 metres high in a tree.

Many baby animals are faced with huge changes that humans have made to their homes. While some animals have adapted to these changes – like the pair of Peregrine Falcons (*Falco peregrinus*) who make their nests at the very top of a Melbourne city skyscraper – many animals experience challenges. Some of the animals you will read about are vulnerable, endangered or critically endangered, making every healthy baby so very important for the survival of their species.

From the tiny to the large, the spikey to the smooth, the social to the shy – we are lucky to have such a diversity of wildlife in our country. So, let's have a look at the wonderful array of baby animals from all across Australia!

Jess Racklyeft

Magpie egg

Chestnut-Backed Buttonquail egg

Spotted Crake egg

Glossy Ibis egg

Banded Stilt egg

Roseate Tern egg

Emu egg

Some useful words you will find in this book

Here are some words and definitions that you might like to know before you read this book. Look out for more definitions through the book.

CLUTCH

The number of eggs laid at one time.

CARNIVORE

An animal that eats other animals.

CRITICALLY ENDANGERED

A species facing an extremely high risk of extinction.

ENDANGERED

A species facing a very high risk of extinction.

ENDEMIC

Found only in a certain place.

GESTATION

Between conception and birth, when the baby is growing inside the womb.

HERBIVORE

An animal that eats plants.

LITTER

The number of animals born to a parent at any one time.

METAMORPHOSIS

The process where an animal develops and changes – for instance, a caterpillar to butterfly, or a tadpole to frog.

For some animals, I have made a decision about the stage of their life that best represents their 'baby' stage. For example, the Hercules Moth *(Coscinocera hercules)* begins life as a larva and then goes through five different instars (developmental moulting stages) before forming a chrysalis (a pupa) and emerging from this cocoon as a giant moth (a whopping 27 cm!).

NOCTURNAL

An animal that is active mostly at night.

VULNERABLE

A species facing a high risk of extinction.

WEANING

When a baby animal stops feeding on milk from its mother.

Classification

All animals can be placed into two main groups: **vertebrates** and **invertebrates**. Vertebrates are animals with a backbone. The main groups (classes) of vertebrates are mammals (including humans!), birds, fish, reptiles and amphibians. Invertebrates do not have a backbone. They include insects, arachnids, molluscs, crustaceans, and animals like corals and sea sponges.

Here are some of the main ways that animals start their lives.

Vertebrates

MAMMALS

Mammal babies grow inside their mother's womb. Once they're born, they feed on milk from their mother's mammary glands.

MARSUPIALS

These mammals are born very tiny and not quite developed, so they need to spend a lot of time growing in their mother's pouch.

MONOTREMES

Platypuses (*Ornithorhynchus anatinus*) and Echidnas (*Tachyglossus aculeatus*) are unusual – they're the only mammals that lay eggs!

BIRDS

Chicks begin life inside an egg that develops inside the mother. Once the egg is laid, a parent keeps it warm and safe in a nest. After hatching, it will grow in stages, from a hatchling to a nestling, a fledgling, a juvenile and finally an adult.

FISH

Most fish lay eggs, which develop outside the mother's body. Hatched eggs produce larvae with yolk sacks that provide the larvae with food. But some live-bearing fish give birth to fry – fully formed baby fish!

REPTILES

Reptile babies mostly hatch from eggs, which are generally laid on land. They are born looking like mini adults, and they behave like them too! These hatchlings are generally independent from the moment they emerge from their eggs.

AMPHIBIANS

Amphibians hatch from soft-skin eggs that have usually been laid in water. They start life as larvae or tadpoles and eventually metamorphose, growing lungs and legs so they can hop onto land!

ARACHNIDS

This group includes spiders and scorpions. Baby spiders hatch from eggs and are known as spiderlings whereas baby scorpions are born live and are known as nymphs.

INSECTS

Insects begin life in eggs and grow into adults in different ways. Some insects, like butterflies and moths, undergo complete metamorphosis, hatching from eggs as larvae and then developing pupae in which they transform into adults.

MOLLUSCS

This group includes snails, slugs, oysters, scallops, mussels and clams. Molluscs hatch from eggs and have different development stages until they reach their adult forms.

CRUSTACEANS

This group includes crabs, lobsters and prawns. These invertebrates hatch from eggs, with some resembling adults at this stage and others developing gradually into adults.

SPONGES

Sea sponges are found in all oceans and in some freshwater environments too. Many sponges start out as larvae and float about before sinking and settling on rocks.

Biomes

There are other ways of classifying animals beyond sorting them as vertebrates and invertebrates. We can group them by species, or more unusual ways such as by their colour, like I did in my book *Australia: Country of Colour*.

In this book, I have grouped the babies by their **biome** – where they spend most of their time, either as a baby or as an adult.

Officially, a biome is an area classified by the kinds of plants, animals, soil and climate found in it. There are different types of biomes: tundra, forest, grassland, marine, freshwater and desert.

I have had fun researching the baby animals of Australia and the environments they might be found – on earth, in trees, in skies, in seas and in rivers.

I hope this book inspires you to take a closer look at the biomes around you and to find out more about the animals and plants that flourish there.

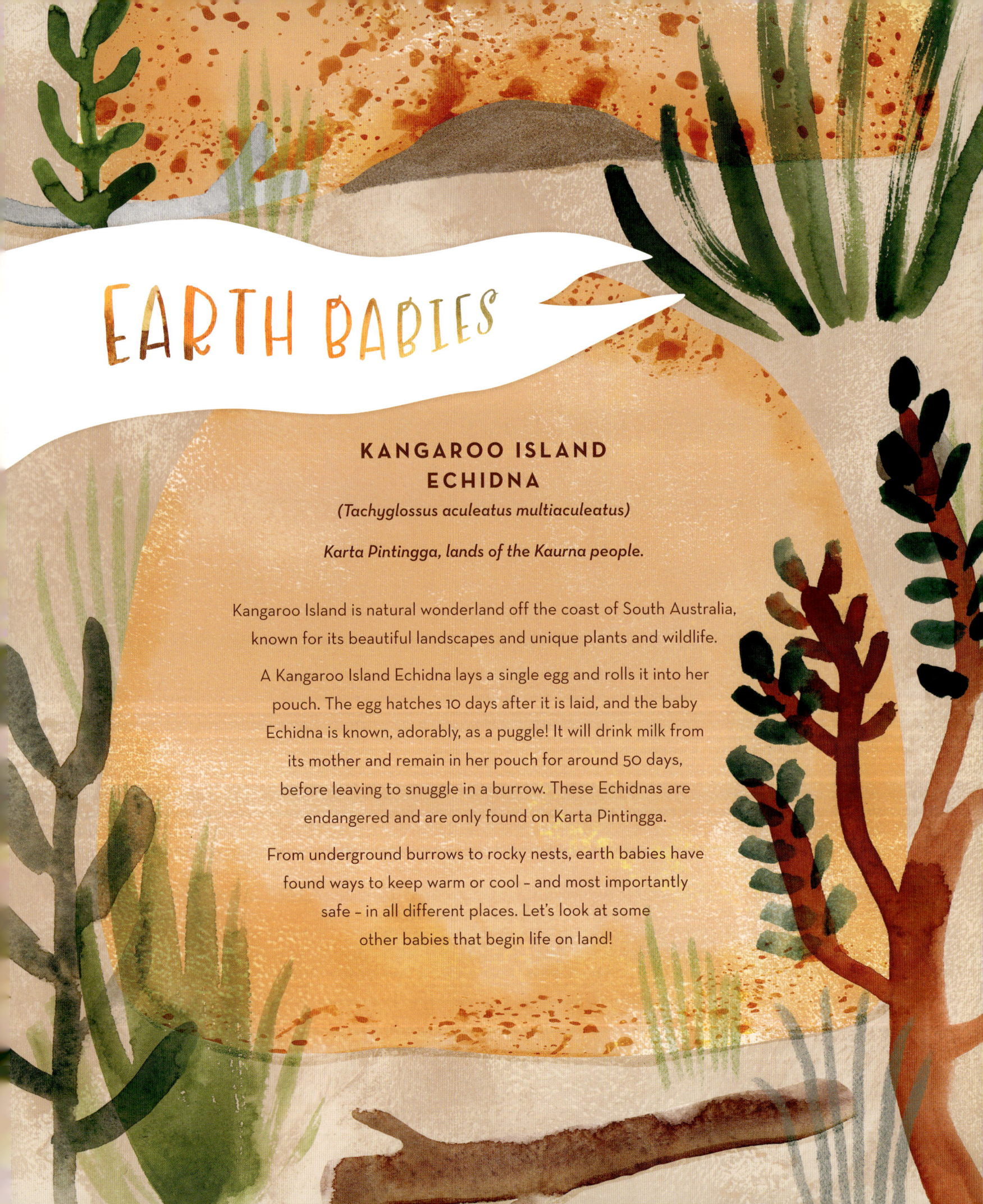

EARTH BABIES

KANGAROO ISLAND ECHIDNA

(Tachyglossus aculeatus multiaculeatus)

Karta Pintingga, lands of the Kaurna people.

Kangaroo Island is natural wonderland off the coast of South Australia, known for its beautiful landscapes and unique plants and wildlife.

A Kangaroo Island Echidna lays a single egg and rolls it into her pouch. The egg hatches 10 days after it is laid, and the baby Echidna is known, adorably, as a puggle! It will drink milk from its mother and remain in her pouch for around 50 days, before leaving to snuggle in a burrow. These Echidnas are endangered and are only found on Karta Pintingga.

From underground burrows to rocky nests, earth babies have found ways to keep warm or cool – and most importantly safe – in all different places. Let's look at some other babies that begin life on land!

SPIDERLING

A baby spider!

Australian Golden Orb-Weaver

(Nephila edulis)

Orb-Weavers build big webs that shine gold in the sun. A female will usually produce just 1 egg sac in her life, but it will contain about 300 eggs! Hatched spiderlings stay close for a few days before heading off to make their own webs.

Land Mullet

(Bellatorias major)

Found mostly in rainforests, these sun-loving skinks give birth to live babies, with 4 to 8 born per season. The babies stay with their mum for a couple of years and will grow quite big – adults can be over 60 cm!

Long-Nosed Bandicoot

(Perameles nasuta)

These small, endangered animals have a gestation period of only 12.5 days – but the joeys spend almost 2 months growing in their mother's pouch!

Antilopine Kangaroo

(Osphranter antilopinus)

A mother will be pregnant for 35 days before giving birth to a joey that will climb up into her pouch and stay there, nice and cosy, for 6 months! Once it emerges, the joey will learn to forage for food in the tropical grasslands.

Furry Tailed Prince

(Anoplognathus flavipennis)

These Christmas Beetles are found along the east coast of Australia. Their eggs are laid underground. Right before Christmas they emerge as adult beetles with spectacular colours!

Spotted-Tailed Quolls

(Dasyurus maculatus)

These endangered marsupials are found on the east coast of Australia. Newborn pups are only the size of a grain of a rice! They will spend weeks latched onto their mother's teat, drinking milk and growing stronger.

Gouldian Finch

(Erythrura gouldiae)

Native to northern Australia, these spectacular birds make their nests in tree hollows or termite mounds, sometimes even sharing their home with other Finch families. Tiny nestlings spend around 3 weeks in their nest before fledging.

NESTLING

A few days after a bird hatches, it is called a nestling – and when it starts flying, it is called a fledgling.

Quokka
(Setonix brachyurus)

Found only in a small part of Western Australia – most famously on Rottnest Island – Quokkas usually give birth to 1 joey at a time, which will stay in its mother's pouch for half a year.

PUP

There are many kinds of pups! Seals, bats, pigs, mice and many more animals have pups.

Greater Bilby *(Macrotis lagotis)*

These long-eared marsupials live in shrubland, rocky soil and deserts. Greater Bilby mums usually have 2 babies who climb into their backwards-facing pouch and stay there for about 80 days.

Pouched Frog

(Assa darlingtoni)

This tiny, vulnerable rainforest frog will lay eggs on land, usually hidden among leaf litter. Newly hatched babies live in a pouch on their dad until they develop into frogs a few months later.

Lord Howe Island Snail

(Varied species)

Lord Howe Island has a diverse ecosystem. Around 70 snail species are found only here, some so rare they were once thought to be extinct! Snails lay tiny eggs, often in big clutches, and newborn snails develop quickly after hatching.

Woylie

(Bettongia penicillata)

Also known as the Brush-Tailed Bettong, these critically endangered marsupials are found in the low grasses and shrublands of Western Australia. A Woylie joey will spend almost 100 days in its mother's pouch.

Bare-Nosed Wombat

(Vombatus ursinus)

A female wombat will carry her joey in her pouch for 5 months. The pouch faces backwards, keeping the joey dirt-free when the wombat digs burrows.

Thorny Devil

(Moloch horridus)

In the arid deserts of Western Australia, female Thorny Devils lay 3 to 10 eggs deep in the hot soil and cover them to keep them safe. After a few months, hatchlings will dig out of their nest. They begin eating ants right away and will eat thousands of ants a day when fully grown!

Superb Lyrebird
(Menura novaehollandiae)

These ancient songbirds are found in bushland and rainforests, where males will create a dancefloor – a mound of bare dirt – and perform a song and dance to attract a mate. Their chick will be looked after by the female in a large nest lined with feathers.

Tasmanian Devil
(Sarcophilus harrisii)

Tasmanian Devil young are called joeys, pups or imps! Mums can give birth to dozens of babies in a litter, but only the few who manage to crawl into her pouch will survive. The pups love to play together – rolling, growling and tumbling.

Long-Nosed Potoroo *(Potorous tridactylus)*

These small members of the kangaroo family live in forests and shrublands, mostly in south-eastern Australia. Joeys emerge from their mums' pouches at around 4 months.

Brushturkey *(Alectura lathami)*

These large birds are known as megapodes as they build their nests in mounds. These nests are a massive, warm pile for their eggs to rest in. Hatchlings will burrow out of the nest fully feathered and almost ready to fly!

HATCHLING

Any baby that has just hatched from an egg, such as tadpoles, baby turtles or newly hatched birds.

Emu
(Dromaius novaehollandiae)

An Emu mum lays between 5 and 15 beautiful eggs, which are kept warm by the father for almost 2 months. The dad emu will barely leave the nest (even for lunch!) and cares for the chicks after they hatch.

Tasmanian Pademelon
(Thylogale billardierii)

Found across Tasmania, these nocturnal herbivores feed on grasses, herbs and flowers. The tiny joeys move to their mother's pouch when they are born and stay there while they grow and develop fur.

Spinifex Hopping Mouse
(Notomys alexis)

These tiny desert creatures keep cool by hiding in burrows during the day and emerging at night. Around 3 to 4 babies are born in each litter, joining several families who live together in the burrows.

Plains-Wanderer
(Pedionomus torquatus)

These critically endangered birds camouflage well within their grassland homes. Once eggs are laid, dads keep them warm and raise the chicks while mums defend the territory.

Broad-toothed Rat
(Mastacomys fuscus)

These chubby-faced rodents are found in Tasmania, southern Victoria and areas of New South Wales. Mothers will have up to 4 babies in summer. They live in nests made of grass, and they eat grass too (so they have green poo!).

Pygmy Copperhead Snake
(Austrelaps labialis)

These small snakes do not lay eggs. Mothers give birth to around 8 snakelets at a time, which are born in sacs. These babies have tiny fangs and are already venomous!

TREE BABIES

VICTORIAN KOALA

(Phascolarctos cinereus victor)

Wye River, lands of the Gadubanud (Katubanut) people.

Wye River is both a town and the name of a waterway that flows into the sea.
It is the gateway to the Great Otway National Park, home to the iconic Golden Wattle
(*Acacia pycnantha*) and many varieties of mighty Eucalyptus.

This tree is a Manna Gum (*Eucalyptus viminalis*) and has a special baby safe in its
branches – a Victorian Koala. There are different subspecies of Koala in Australia, and
the Victorian Koala is the largest. But Koala babies are born very tiny! A newborn joey
weighs less than a gram and will look like a pink jellybean. After staying in the pouch and
drinking milk for around six months, the joey will be ready to see the world. Its mum will
begin feeding it a kind of poo called pap – a special food that helps the joey get ready for
a Eucalyptus diet. By nine months, the joey can ride on its mother's back.

Tree-dwelling animals are also known as arboreal animals. Let's keep our eyes
peeled for Australia's arboreal animals and their babies!

Common Ringtail Possum

(Pseudocheirus peregrinus)

These possums live in large, busy nests called dreys. Often the mum, dad, joeys and older offspring live in the same drey! This is the only species of possum where dads will help care for joeys. When the mother is off finding food, the father will carry the babies on his back.

Wompoo Fruit-Dove

(Ptilinopus magnificus)

These birds are found high in the trees along Australia's east coast and can be recognised by their distinctive call and bright colours. A mum will lay 1 egg per season and will share duties with the dad, from building a nest to looking after the chick.

Golden Brushtail Possum

(Trichosurus vulpecula)

These beautiful possums are gold because of a rare genetic mutation, and their fur makes it hard for them to hide from predators in their tree homes. Once a joey emerges from its mum's pouch, it will take rides on her back, seeing the world from a safe viewpoint.

Leadbeater's Possum

(Gymnobelideus leadbeateri)

These tiny, critically endangered possums live with their family group in tree-hollow dreys. Mothers have only 1 to 2 babies per litter. Once thought to be extinct, a small population can be found in pockets of ash forests and woodlands in Victoria.

NYMPHS

The young form of some insects and other invertebrates.

Steel-Blue Sawfly

(Perga dorsalis)

This wasp-like insect's larvae are often found in big clusters on Eucalyptus trees and are known as spitfires because they spit out goopy liquid when threatened.

Tawny Frogmouth

(Podargus strigoides)

Found perched in trees across almost all of Australia, these big birds camouflage perfectly against tree branches. The mum and dad will partner for life and will take turns keeping their eggs warm in the nest and feeding their fluffy hatchlings.

Gang-Gang Cockatoo

(Callocephalon fimbriatum)

Gang-Gangs use their strong beaks to strip bark and make snuggly nests with it in tree hollows. Families will often roost together in the same tree and sometimes form a kind of daycare, with a few parents watching the chicks while others forage for food.

Lesser Long-Eared Bat

(Nyctophilus geoffroyi)

These little bats can be found in old tree hollows or caves. They usually live alone, but pregnant females will group together in spring. Mums usually give birth to twin pups who will roost for up to 6 weeks and then begin hunting and flying.

JOEY

A baby kangaroo, but also the name for other marsupial babies, such as wombats, possums and koalas.

Long-Tailed Pygmy Possum

(Cercartetus caudatus)

These tiny possums are found in the rainforests of northern Australia. Mums can give birth to up to 8 joeys a year, but they live in nests at such high altitudes that not much is known about them!

Boyd's Forest Dragon *(Lophosaurus boydii)*

Found in the rainforests of tropical northern Queensland, these tree-dwelling lizards rest sleepily until prey wanders by. Females lay a clutch of up to 6 eggs in shallow nests, and babies take about a year to grow to adult size.

Green Tree Snake

(Dendrelaphis punctulatus)

These snakes rest in trees but hide in grass and rocks when hunting. They are not venomous but can emit a stink to scare away threats! A female will lay 5 to 12 eggs per clutch and will wrap them with her body to keep them warm.

SNAKELET

A baby snake!

Black-Footed Tree-Rat

(Mesembriomys gouldii)

These endangered nocturnal rats are found in the north of Australia and are one of our largest native rodents. They shelter in tree hollows during the day, and at night they come out to hunt. A baby rat is known as a pinkie, kit or pup!

Huntsman Spider

(Isopeda montana)

These large spiders like to keep cosy under bark or woodpiles. The female will lay flat oval eggs and guard them for 3 weeks, without even leaving to find food! Once the spiderlings hatch, she will remain with them for weeks to keep them safe.

Green Tree Ants

(Oecophylla smaragdina)

A queen ant lays her eggs, and then her young larvae are carried off by worker ants. The larvae produce a kind of silk, and workers will use this to bind leaves together and make incredible nests.

Spiny Leaf Insect
(Extatosoma tiaratum)

These large insects can be found dining on leaves in rainforests. Females lay their eggs and then flick them onto the forest floor. When the nymphs hatch, they look like poisonous ants, which helps them avoid predators – no one wants to eat them!

Greater Glider
(Petauroides volans)

These endangered gliders live in old Eucalyptus trees along the east coast of Australia. At night, they forage for food between trees – adults can glide a whopping 100 m, and joeys will join them in gliding at about 9 months old.

Green Tree Frog
(Ranoidea caerulea)

Mothers lay their eggs in puddles or ponds. The eggs clump together in a cluster known as frogspawn and will float like a raft. The tiny tadpoles are under 1 cm long, but they'll grow into big frogs – up to a whopping 11 cm.

Gumleaf Skeletoniser
(Uraba lugens)

These furry grey moths lay up to 200 eggs on Eucalyptus leaves. Once they reach caterpillar stage, they moult many times, keeping the exoskeletons of their heads stacked like hats, earning their nickname of mad hatterpillars!

Squirrel Glider (Petaurus norfolcensis)

Usually found where iron-bark Eucalyptus is plentiful, these small possums spend most of their lives high up in the trees. Two babies usually stay in their mother's pouch for 70 days.

Bennett's Tree-Kangaroo

(Dendrolagus bennettianus)

Found in tree canopies in Far North Queensland, these macropods can jump as far as 9 m across the treetops! Newborn joeys are the size of jellybeans, but at around 2 years they'll be big enough to find their own trees to graze and jump from.

Red Gum Lerp Psyllid

(Glycaspis brimblecombei)

Females lay orangey-yellow eggs on the leaves of red gum trees. From the eggs hatch nymphs, which will cover themselves in a crystalised honeydew known as lerp until they're ready to emerge as adults.

Honey Possum

(Tarsipes rostratus)

Also known as Noolbengers, these tiny possums are found only in Western Australia. Newborn Noolbengers are the smallest of all baby mammals, each weighing about the same as a grain of salt!

SKY BABIES

ULYSSES BUTTERFLY

(Papilio ulysses)

Daintree Rainforest, lands of the Eastern Kuku Yalanji people.

The Daintree in tropical North Queensland is the largest rainforest in Australia, and one of the oldest rainforests in the world. It's home to many creatures that are found nowhere else on Earth.

The spectacular Ulysses Butterfly begins life as an egg laid on the leaf of the Euodia tree (*Melicope elleryana*). After hatching and developing into a young caterpillar, it will spend its day resting on leaves, its green colour helping to disguise it from predators. When it's ready, the caterpillar will form a chrysalis, or pupa, and then finally emerge as a stunning blue butterfly with iridescent wings spanning up to 14 cm!

Australian skies are filled with incredible animals – around 800 species of birds as well as Flying Foxes and thousands of insects. Baby flying animals might not be found sky-high right away though, so let's look at the early days before they take flight.

Swift Parrot
(Lathamus discolor)

These critically endangered parrots breed in tree holes close to their favourite flowering Eucalyptus. Their young are fed delicious nectar from these flowers.

Peregrine Falcon *(Falco peregrinus)*

These excellent flyers are found all over the world, and there's even a pair that nest on a Melbourne skyscraper! Both parents will care for their young; they sometimes drop food from the air, encouraging the juveniles to fly, dive and hunt!

Pellucid Hawk Moth
(Cephonodes hylas)

These common moths start life in pale green eggs, and when metamorphosis is complete, they will emerge with stunning green, yellow and black bodies and transparent wings.

Shy Albatross

(Thalassarche cauta)

The Shy Albatross mum will lay a single egg on a nest made from dirt and grass, and she will care for her chick for 5 months before it fledges. These birds breed on islands off Tasmania, but they can fly all the way to South Africa, with wingspans of up to 2.6 m!

Blue Banded Bee

(Amegilla cingulata)

These native bees are unique: they are solitary, they live in burrows, and they don't make honey! Mothers lay their eggs with a little picnic left underneath them – a mix of nectar and pollen that is eaten by the larvae after hatching.

Laughing Kookaburra

(Dacelo novaeguineae)

Found in most of eastern Australia's forests and woodlands, families of Laughing Kookaburras can be large – nests might house 3 eggs and up to 5 older siblings, who will help raise the babies with their parents!

Imperial Hairstreak Butterfly

(Jalmenus evagoras)

This butterfly's eggs are laid in clumps and have a unique spiky appearance. During its instar stage, it has a close relationship with black ants, which help defend it from predators before it transforms into a beautiful butterfly.

INSTARS

For some insects, such as caterpillars, this is a stage of development that occurs between moults (when the insect sheds its skin).

Regent Honeyeater

(Anthochaera phrygia)

These critically endangered birds are found in the woodlands of Victoria and New South Wales, where they'll make nests of bark, twigs and grass, ready to house up to 3 eggs. Regent Honeyeaters are excellent mimics of other honeyeaters, but sadly there are so few of them left that some have forgotten their own song.

Eastern Curlew *(Numenius madagascariensis)*

This critically endangered bird is found on the shorelines of Australia, but, incredibly, it will migrate 10,000 km to breed – all the way to Russia, Siberia and China! It begins its life in the boggy marshes of these countries and is independent from birth, migrating to Australia alone from only 6 weeks of age!

Rainbow Lorikeet

(Trichoglossus moluccanus)

Found over much of Australia, these noisy birds are recognised by their vibrant feathers. Rainbow Lorikeet nestlings are mostly grey with flecks of the rainbow colours they will soon develop all over.

JUVENILE

The stage of development before an animal reaches reproductive maturity.

Powerful Owl *(Ninox strenua)*

The largest Australian owl, Powerful Owls mate for life and can be together for as long as 30 years. They make nests in the hollows of big, old trees, where females will lay two eggs at a time. The young will normally spend 7 weeks in the cosy nest, but some may live with their parents for a year.

Pied Currawong

(Strepera graculina)

These crow-like birds are found along the east coast and can be recognised by their distinctive call. Pied Currawongs are born featherless and blind but soon grow fluffy down, then feathers, and develop sharp eyesight.

Grey-Headed Flying Fox
(Pteropus poliocephalus)

These are the largest bats in Australia, with wingspans of almost 1 m. They are nature's helpers – distributing seeds for different plants across the land. Females usually have 1 baby per year, which will cling to its mother for its first few weeks, drinking milk and staying warm.

Bogong Moth
(Agrotis infusa)

Females lay around 2,000 eggs in the soil. The larvae, known as Black Cutworms, emerge from underground in spring. Eventually they'll sprout wings and migrate 1,000 km to the Australian Alps, often in swarms of thousands.

Spectacled Flying Fox
(Pteropus conspicillatus)

These endangered bats are found in Queensland and on nearby islands. One pup is born each year and will stay close to its mum for months. Eventually, juveniles will spend time in nursery trees with other young flying foxes before they venture afield.

Wedge-Tailed Eagle (Aquila audax)

The biggest bird-of-prey in Australia, these eagles make nests in the tallest trees in their territory so that they have the best views! Their giant nests can weigh hundreds of kilograms but will usually hold just 1 or 2 eggs. Hatchlings are born fluffy and develop feathers 50 days or so later.

AUSTRALIAN FUR SEAL

(Arctocephalus pusillus doriferus)

Tenth Island, Tasmania (Roobala mangana). Sea and waters of the palawa-pakana people.

Near the north coast of Tasmania is a tiny, rocky island that has no trees or plants. This island is uninhabited by humans but is a thriving home for a colony of Australian Fur Seals (*Arctocephalus pusillus doriferus*).

Female Fur Seals will come ashore to join their colony just before the birth of their babies. Pups are born in summer and will spend their first few weeks with their mum, drinking her milk. Then, mums will go hunting out in the water for a few days before returning to shore. A mother seal can find her baby among the crowd by its distinct call.

Australia is the largest island in the world, and features some of the most amazing sea life found anywhere on Earth! From the colourful Great Barrier Reef to the turquoise seas of Esperance, the calm Timor Sea in the north to the tumultuous Tasman Sea in the south, sea babies are found on the shores, shallows and depths. Let's have a splash and take a closer look!

SEA BABIES

Australian Flat Oyster

(Ostrea angasi)

Also known as the southern mud oyster, these molluscs are found on the sandy bottoms of coastal waters in southern Australia. Oyster larvae settle into rocky places and take a year to mature.

Red Handfish

(Thymichthys politus)

There are now fewer than 100 or so Red Handfish in the wild, found only on patches of reef in Tasmania. Females lay eggs at the bottom of seaweed and guard the eggs until they hatch.

Maugean Skate

(Zearaja maugeana)

This endangered ancient skate now lives only in the Macquarie Harbour in Tasmania. Females lay leathery eggs that sink to the silty harbour floor and hatch 31 weeks later. The young skates will resemble tiny versions of their parents.

Humpback Whale

(Megaptera novaeangliae)

Humpback Whales migrate from Antarctic seas to warm northern waters, travelling up to 10,000 km! Their calves are giant – between 3 m and 5 m at birth – and will feed on milk for several months. Whale calves love playing and exploring.

Hooded Plover

(Thinornis rubricollis)

The vulnerable Hooded Plover nests on beaches and coastlines, where females lay up to 3 eggs in the sand above the high-tide line. While both parents incubate the eggs, their nests are at high risk of being disturbed by predators and humans.

Nudibranch

(Nembrotha purpureolineata)

Also called sea slugs, these molluscs are mostly found in warm, tropical waters. Newly hatched Nudibranchs have small shells that eventually fall off, revealing the spectacular colours underneath.

Reef Manta Ray

(Mobula alfredi)

Found in warm, tropical waters, females will give birth every couple of years to 1 live pup who is immediately ready to live on its own. These rays can grow up to 5 m in diameter and can live for over 50 years!

Tiger Snout Seahorse

(Hippocampus subelongatus)

Found only in the waters of south-western Australia, Tiger Snout Seahorse mums give their eggs to the dads, who carry them in their pouches until the fry are born.

FINGERLING

A juvenile fish – they are usually around the size of a finger!

Snubfin Dolphin

(Orcaella heinsohni)

Found in the north of Australia, usually in shallow areas close to river mouths, these dolphins make clicks, whistles and pulsing sounds to communicate with their group. Calves drink milk from their mums for around 2 years before becoming independent.

Blobfish

(Psychrolutes marcidus)

These flabby fish are found deep in the ocean. Their bodies are not always so floppy though – they lose shape the closer they rise to the surface. Females lay thousands of eggs, and when larvae hatch, they look like mini blobs!

Little Penguin

(Eudyptula minor)

These tiny seabirds are found only on Australia's southern coast and in New Zealand. Males dig burrows and females lay up to 2 eggs in them, with both parents sharing incubation. Chicks have black, fluffy down, which is eventually replaced by dense waterproof feathers.

Sea Star

(Asterodiscides truncates)

Found in many marine environments, from shallow beaches to deep oceans, Sea Stars start life on the sea floor, eventually growing into their incredible star form.

Terek Sandpiper
(Xenus cinereus)

Terek Sandpipers spend August until March hunting in the wetlands of Australia before they migrate for their breeding season in the cold tundras of Russia and Finland. Parents work together, with dads defending the nest and mums keeping their eggs warm.

FRY

The juvenile stage for many water animals.

Rose Sponge
(Dendrilla rosea)

Living in oceans or rocky reefs, these pretty sponges are a simple kind of animal with few predators. Their larvae settle on the sea floor or rocky outcrops where they become new sea sponges.

Grey Nurse Shark
(Carcharias taurus)

Mums make a long migration from warm waters to cooler waters to give birth and usually have two pups in a litter. Pups are over 1 m in length at birth and quickly grow to over 3 times that size.

White-Bellied Sea-Eagle
(Haliaeetus leucogaster)

Found around Australia's coasts and near other waterways, these large raptors start life in huge nests found high in trees or on cliffs. Juveniles have brown feathers but develop striking white and grey adult feathers by their fourth year.

LARVA

An immature form of an animal in-between the egg and pupa phase, or the early stage before metamorphosis, such as the tadpole stage.

Dwarf Sawfish

(Pristis clavata)

Found in tropical northern Australia, these vulnerable fish can live a long time – up to 48 years! Eggs develop inside the mums, and the growing embryos feed on the yolk of their eggs before they are born.

Eastern Gobbleguts

(Vincentia novaehollandiae)

The Eastern Gobbleguts dad holds the fertilised eggs in his mouth for about 2 weeks until they hatch, a process known as mouthbrooding.

Spiny Sea Urchin

(Centrostephanus rodgersii)

Spiny Sea Urchin larvae are called zooplankton. There are typically large amounts of zooplankton, but only a small number find a spot to rest and grow. To do this, they turn themselves inside out and soon resemble their better-known spiky adult form.

Great Barrier Reef Clownfish

(Amphiprion akindynos)

Clownfish eggs are guarded by the dads, who will look after the babies when they hatch. All Clownfish are born male, but some turn female later on. These fish live among anemones, whom they have a symbiotic relationship with.

Bump-Head Sunfish

(Mola alexandrini)

These fish can grow to more than 3 m in length, but they begin life as tiny larvae under 2 mm long. As the fry grow, they develop their head bump and other features, like their dorsal fin, which can make them look like sharks!

Flatback Turtle

(Natator depressus)

Females lay eggs in sandy beach nests, and the temperature of the sand helps determine the sex of the babies. If the sand is below 29°C, males are born, and above 29°C, the turtles will be female. Hatchlings dig their way out of their nest before heading out to sea.

Dugong

(Dugong dugon)

Found in shallow warm waters among seagrasses, these gentle giants are also known as sea cows. A female will have 1 calf per litter, and it will be over 1 m long! The mother will push the calf to the surface to breathe.

CALF

The name for baby whales, dugongs and dolphins (and cows!).

Leafy Sea Dragon

(Phycodurus eques)

Leafy Sea Dragon eggs start out pink, and the dad will carry them around on his tail. When the eggs turn orange, he will rub his tail on seaweed and rocks to encourage the babies to hatch. Baby seahorses, called fry, are independent from birth.

RIVER BABIES

PLATYPUS

(Ornithorhynchus anatinus)

Guula Ngurra National Park, lands of the Gundungurra people.

Nestled alongside the Wingecarribee and Wollondilly Rivers is one of Australia's newest national parks. Steep, rocky gullies drop spectacularly into the river valleys, and the place where the two rivers meet holds particular significance to the Gundungurra people.

Rivers and waterways are so varied across Australia, and they change throughout the year according to weather, rainfall and water flow.

Platypuses are found in many of our waterways on the east coast of Australia. These unique mammals lay eggs. Along with Echidnas, they are the world's only egg-laying mammals!

When nesting, the mother Platypus makes a long burrow – up to 20 metres in length – and lines it with leaves. She will usually lay two eggs, keeping them warm by wrapping herself around them. Her babies are known as puggles and are fed milk through pores on her skin. After about 5 months, they leave their burrow to experience more of river life.

From the Platypus to the Pobblebonk, there are plenty of river babies to meet! Let's discover some of the unique animals that begin life in or near our mighty rivers, creeks and streams.

Giant Water Bug
(Lethocerus insulanus)

These big bugs are found in freshwater all around Australia. The female lays around 80 eggs at a time, and the male will carry the eggs on his back until they hatch. These bugs use a kind of snorkel on their rear end to breathe when they are hunting!

Freshwater Crayfish
(Cherax quadricarinatus)

Found in the north of Australia, female Freshwater Crayfish lay hundreds of olive-coloured eggs, which attach to her tail when fertilised. Around 6 weeks later, the juveniles hatch and are soon ready to fend for themselves.

Little Egret *(Egretta garzetta)*

These birds are found in wetlands all over Australia, from saltmarshes to tidal mudflats. They make nests in reeds or bushes near the water, with the dad bringing supplies for the mum to build the nest. Parents take turns minding the eggs, and their hatchlings will be fluffy.

Blue Mountains Tree Frog

(Ranoidea citropa)

Living around rocky streams in the Blue Mountains, these frogs lay over 600 eggs in clutches. Hatched tadpoles are gold-coloured and take a couple of months to develop into froglets, changing colour as they grow.

Freshwater Crocodile

(Crocodylus johnstoni)

Freshwater Crocodiles are found in waterways across the north of Australia. Mums lay their eggs in sandy chambers. When young crocs are ready to hatch, they call out from within their eggs! Mums will help to open the eggs and will carry the babies to the water in their mouths.

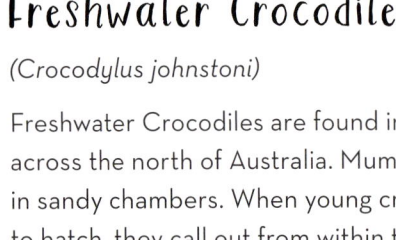

Black Swan
(Cygnus artratus)

Black Swans make their nests in reeds near wetlands, rivers and lakes. Parents take turns looking after baby swans, called cygnets.

Southern Purple-Spotted Gudgeon
(Mogurnda adspersa)

Found in a variety of waterways, these endangered fish prefer calm rivers and creeks. The mum lays eggs on underwater plants and rocks, and the dad will guard the eggs.

Rakali *(Hydromys chrysogaster)*

These native water rats are found near all bodies of water, from creeks to the sea. Rakali make their nests in burrows, but in urban areas they have adapted their nests to suit different places, even drainpipes! Rakali mums have up to four pups in a litter. The pups will drink milk for around a month until they can find their own food.

Short Headed Lamprey
(Mordacia mordax)

These fish spend most of their life in the sea but head to freshwater rivers to breed. Females lay thousands of small eggs, which hatch into worm-like juveniles. They take around 3 years to metamorphose into adults before migrating to the sea.

PUGGLE

Platypus and Echidna babies have this adorable name.

Mary River Turtle
(Elusor macrurus)

This endangered turtle is famous for its green punk-style hair – which is actually algae sprouting from its head! They are only found in the Mary River in Queensland. Parents begin breeding when they are over 25 years old and will dig nests on sun-facing riverbanks.

Sacred Kingfisher
(Todiramphus sanctus)

These eye-catching birds begin life in a riverbank burrow or termite mound. Both parents look after the young, and juveniles have usually developed striking green-blue feathers by the time they've fledged.

Barred Galaxias *(Galaxias fuscus)*

These endangered fish are only found in a few streams in Victoria. Little is known about how they start life, but it is assumed they spawn in spring, with larvae growing into juvenile fish over a couple of months.

Australian Pelican

(Pelecanus conspicillatus)

Australian Pelicans nest in colonies, with most found on islands off South Australia. Their hatchlings are born featherless, and the first to hatch will be the largest of the siblings. By the time they're adults they will have a massive wingspan of up to 2.6 m!

Fitzroy River Turtle

(Rheodytes leukops)

These vulnerable turtles are only found in the waterways of the Fitzroy River. Females lay eggs in nests on the riverbank. They are known as bum-breathing turtles as they can breathe through gills in their bums!

Murray Cod

(Maccullochella peelii)

The largest freshwater fish in Australia begins life as a tiny egg laid in spring. Dads will guard the eggs and watch over the larvae for their first week after hatching.

Blue-Billed Duck
(Oxyura australis)

These ducks spend most of their lives on the water of lakes or swamps – they are quite clumsy on land! Their bowl-shaped nests hold 5 to 6 eggs, and chicks will grow to adult-sized within 2 months of hatching.

Tasmanian Giant Freshwater Crayfish

(Astacopsis gouldi)

Found in Tasmanian rivers, these vulnerable crayfish are the largest freshwater crays in the world. A female will lay hundreds of eggs, which she will carry on her tail. Hatchlings will stay attached to her legs for months, then they will slowly grow and grow.

PUPA

The insect stage after larva and before the insect becomes an adult. This is often at the stage of a cocoon; for instance, when a caterpillar is becoming a butterfly.

Common Bluetail Damselfly

(Ischnura heterosticta)

Damselfly larvae are sometimes called Mud Eyes. They feed on small insects in the water and go through several stages before emerging as an adult.

Pobblebonk

(Limnodynastes dumerilii)

This burrowing frog is found across Victoria and is known for its excellent call. A female can lay up to 4,000 eggs at a time! She will use her arms to beat her egg clutches, stirring a foam around them that creates a floating raft.

Olive Perchlet *(Ambassis agassizii)*

Found in rivers, creeks, ponds and swamps, these tiny fish breed when the water warms. Females lay up to 700 eggs, which attach to plants and rocks underwater. Larvae are just 3 mm long, but they begin swimming and feeding by the time they are a week old.

Australian Smelt

(Retropinna semoni)

These common freshwater fish are found in huge schools, particularly in lakes but also in rivers and wetlands. They spawn in spring, with females laying hundreds of thousands of transparent eggs in a batch.

All of the creatures in this book are wild animals and are found in the amazing diverse environments around us in Australia. They are definitely not pets!

So how can you help them?

The best way to support the lives of our native animals is to help protect their habitats. We need to preserve the biomes where they live – the forests, deserts, mountains, rivers, streams, ocean and sky as best we can. You may have noticed some of the babies in the book are listed as vulnerable, endangered or even critically endangered. This means that there are few of them left in the wild, and that they are facing threats to their survival.

There are lots of wonderful groups who work hard to help support Australia's natural environments. Here are some groups you might like to look up and support:

Seed Mob
www.seedmob.org.au

BirdLife Australia
www.birdlife.org.au

Australian Wildlife Conservancy
www.australianwildlife.org

Bush Heritage Australia
www.bushheritage.org.au

If you ever find injured wildlife, there are several experienced organisations you can ask for help. They can advise you if the wildlife is safe to be moved. Here are a few:

Victoria
www.wildlifevictoria.org.au

South Australia
www.faunarescue.org.au

New South Wales
www.nwc.org.au/resources/injured-wildlife-find-your-nearest-rescue-group

Tasmania
www.bonorong.com.au/wildlife-rescue-service

Western Australia
www.wawildlife.org.au

Australian Capital Territory
www.actwildlife.net

Northern Territorry
www.dwsnt.com.au

Queensland
phone 1300 ANIMAL (1300 264 625)

For non-native animals, try asking the RSPCA or a local vet for help.

In little ways, we can all try to be as environmentally friendly as possible. Recycling, reusing materials, and not wasting what we have is a wonderful start. You could also try making a compost heap in your garden (the perfect place for many bugs to eat, breed and have babies!). You could make a bee hotel or plant native flora in your garden to encourage birds and bees to visit. And you can keep old trees growing tall and strong, as they can be homes for so many animal families. At the beach or river, take all your rubbish home with you, and even collect other rubbish you might find washed up on the shore.